D0484106

JANE AUSTEN

First published in the United States in 2016
by Chronicle Books LLC.
Text copyright © 2016 by Zena Alkayat.
Illustrations copyright © 2016 by Nina Cosford.
All rights reserved. No part of this book may be
reproduced in any form without written
permission from the publisher.

Library of Congress Cataloging-in-Publication
Data available.

ISBN: 978-1-4521-5021-5

Manufactured in China.

First published in the UK by Frances Lincoln Ltd.

10 9 8 7 6 5 4 3 2 1

Chronicle Books LLC
680 Second Street
San Francisco, CA 94107

www.chroniclebooks.com

JANE AUSTEN

by Zena Alkayat and Nina Cosford

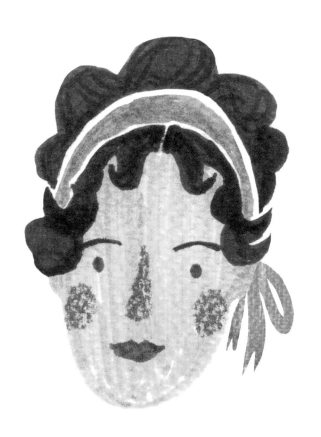

"Which of all my important nothings shall I tell you first?"

Letter, 1808

JANE AUSTEN WAS BORN ON DECEMBER 16, 1775, IN STEVENTON, HAMPSHIRE. SHE LIVED IN THE VILLAGE RECTORY WITH HER FATHER, GEORGE, AND MOTHER, CASSANDRA.

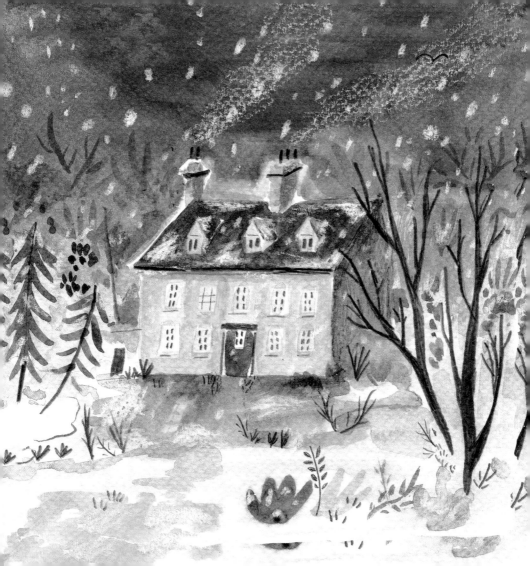

THE RECTORY WAS ALSO A
WORKING FARM, COMPLETE WITH
COWS, CHICKENS, AND DUCKS, AS
WELL AS WHEAT, BARLEY, AND HOPS.
JANE GREW UP WITH SIX BROTHERS
AND ONE SISTER.

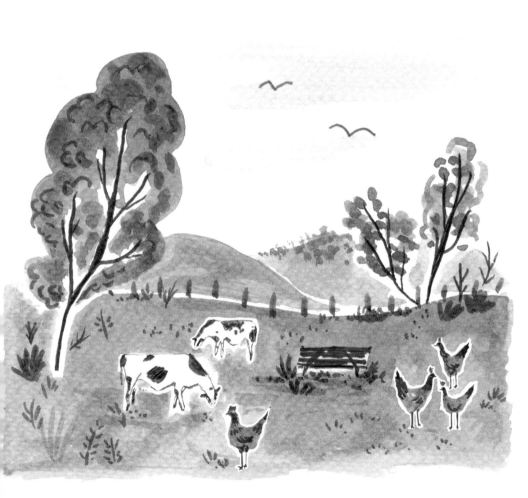

The Austen

Rev. George Austen

James
Austen

George
Austen

Edward
Austen

Henry
Austen

Family Tree

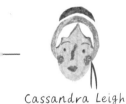

Cassandra Leigh

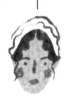

Cassandra
Austen

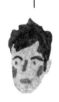

Francis "Frank"
Austen

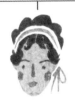

Jane
Austen

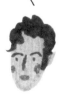

Charles
Austen

JANE'S FATHER WAS A PARSON AND A FARMER, BUT TO SUPPLEMENT HIS FAMILY'S INCOME, HE AND MRS. AUSTEN TURNED THE RECTORY INTO A SMALL BOYS' BOARDING SCHOOL.

SO JANE WAS USED TO
BEING AROUND MALE COMPANY —
AND LOTS AND LOTS OF BOOKS.

AS YOUNG CHILDREN, JANE AND
CASSANDRA WERE INSEPARABLE.
THE SISTERS WENT TO BOARDING
SCHOOL TOGETHER WHERE THEY
LEARNED SPELLING, FRENCH, MATH,
NEEDLEWORK, AND DANCE.

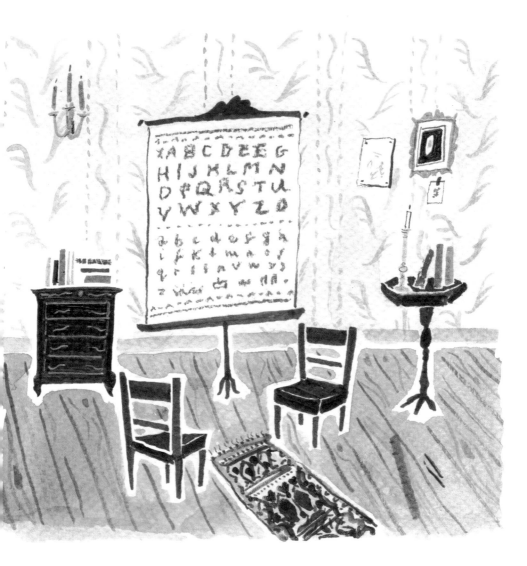

WHEN JANE WAS ELEVEN, HER COUSIN ELIZA CAME TO SPEND CHRISTMAS AT STEVENTON. ELIZA WAS MYSTERIOUS AND STRIKING, AND HER LIFE WAS AS FANTASTICAL AS FICTION. SHE WAS MARRIED TO A EUROPEAN COUNT, SPOKE FLUENT FRENCH, AND WORE CONTINENTAL FASHIONS.

HER GLAMOUR CAUSED A STIR: THE AUSTEN BOYS FLIRTED, AND JANE FOUND A LIFELONG FRIEND.

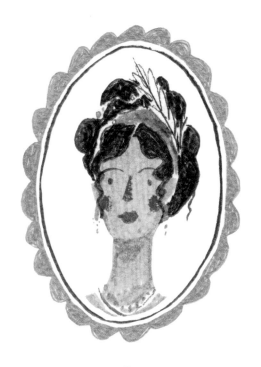

Eliza

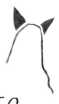

THE AUSTENS LOVED TO
PUT ON PLAYS.

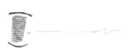

THEY INVITED FRIENDS TO TAKE ON
ROLES AND PAINTED SETS AND PROPS
FOR THEIR PRODUCTIONS.

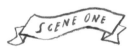

SCENE ONE

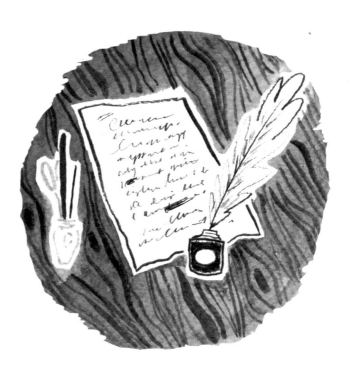

THEY ALSO LOVED TO WRITE.
JANE'S MOTHER WROTE VERSE,
AND HER BROTHER JAMES WAS
A SKILLED POET. JANE PREFERRED
PROSE AND FILLED NOTEBOOKS
WITH WILD AND WITTY STORIES.

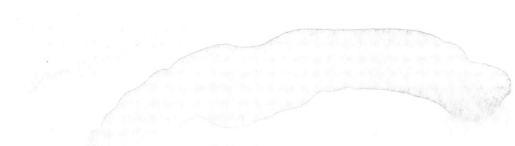

ALL AROUND HER, PEOPLE WERE GETTING MARRIED. AND THE SUBJECT OF MONEY WAS NEVER FAR AWAY.

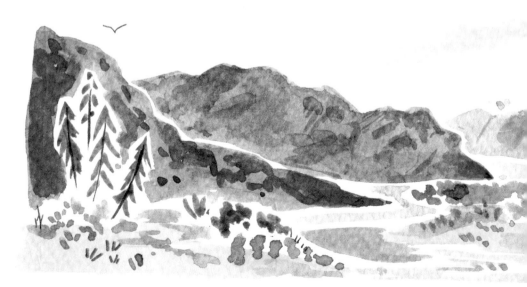

JANE HEARD HOW COUSIN ELIZA
WAS BORN IN INDIA AFTER HER
MOTHER WENT THERE DETERMINED
TO FIND A HUSBAND AMONG
THE ENGLISH TRADERS.

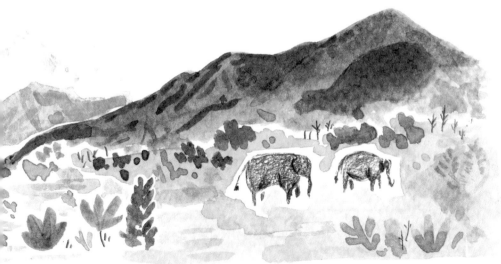

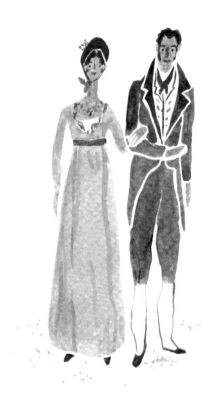

CASSANDRA WAS SOON ENGAGED TO A YOUNG CLERGYMAN NAMED THOMAS FOWLE. BUT NEITHER HAD ANY MONEY, AND A MARRIAGE WAS UNLIKELY TO BE ARRANGED WITHOUT IT.

BY HER LATE TEENS, JANE HAD
BEGUN WORK ON A NOVELLA.

"LADY SUSAN" WAS ABOUT A
SCHEMING WOMAN ON THE
HUNT FOR TWO HUSBANDS, ONE
FOR HERSELF, ANOTHER FOR
HER DAUGHTER.

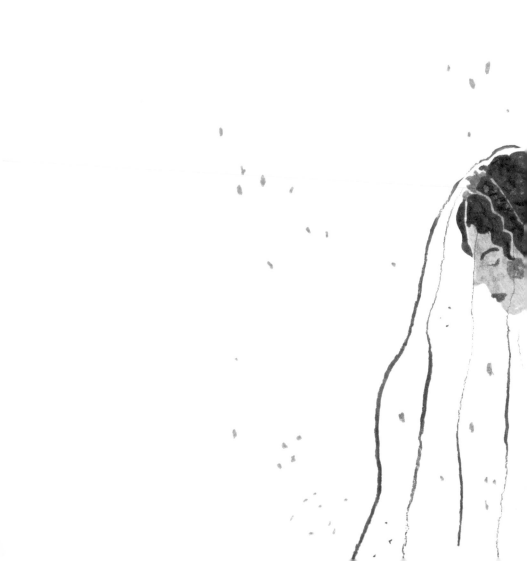

IT DIDN'T TAKE LONG FOR
JANE'S FAMILY TO RECOGNIZE
HER EXTRAORDINARY TALENT.
HER FATHER WAS EXCEPTIONALLY
PROUD AND BOUGHT HER A SMALL
MAHOGANY WRITING TABLE FOR
HER NINETEENTH BIRTHDAY.

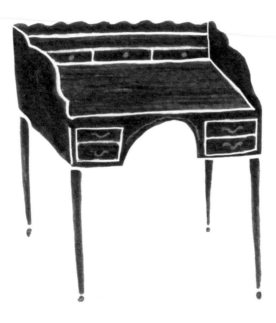

JANE LOVED TO DANCE AND ATTENDED BALLS HOSTED BY THE GENTRY IN THE VILLAGE.

THE FURNITURE WOULD BE PUSHED BACK, A NEIGHBOR MIGHT PICK UP HIS FIDDLE, AND SOMEONE WOULD PLAY THE PIANO.

"To be fond of dancing was a certain step towards falling in love."

"Pride and Prejudice", 1813

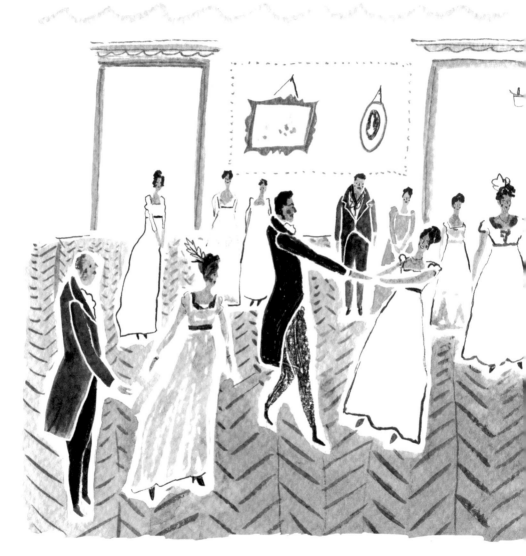

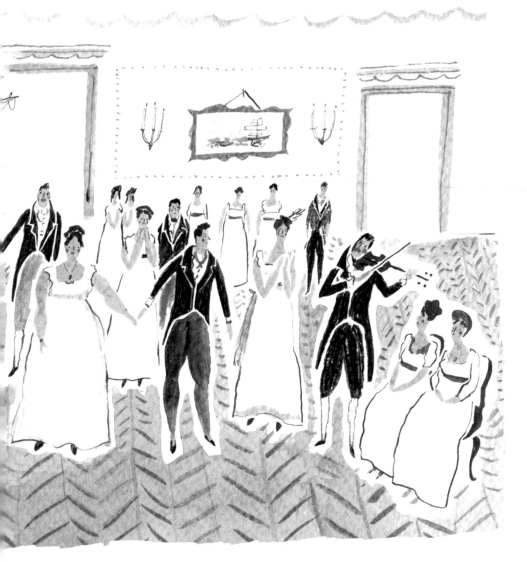

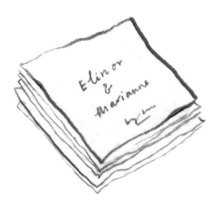

JANE HAD A GIFT FOR SOCIAL OBSERVATION AND A SHARP EYE FOR HUMAN FOLLY. NOT YET TWENTY, SHE BEGAN WRITING HER FIRST NOVEL "ELINOR AND MARIANNE", WHICH WENT ON TO BECOME "SENSE AND SENSIBILITY".

MEANWHILE THE BATTLES OF
THE FRENCH REVOLUTION WERE
BEING WAGED. ENGLISH CAVALRYMEN
WERE NEEDED AND FOUR OF JANE'S
BROTHERS WERE INVOLVED IN THE
MILITARY AND THE NAVY.

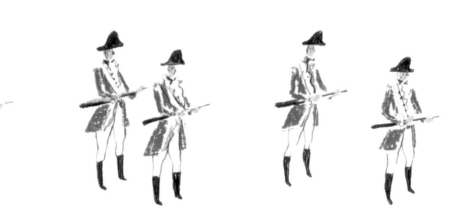

COUSIN ELIZA'S HUSBAND WAS KILLED IN FRANCE, LEAVING HER WIDOWED WITH A SMALL CHILD.

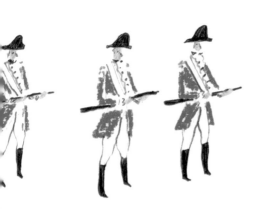
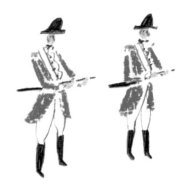

APART FROM A GROWING NUMBER OF OFFICERS AROUND TOWN, LIFE IN STEVENTON REMAINED UNCHANGED. JANE CONTINUED TO FLIRT AND DANCE WITH ELIGIBLE YOUNG MEN—AND THEN SHE MET LAW STUDENT TOM LEFROY.

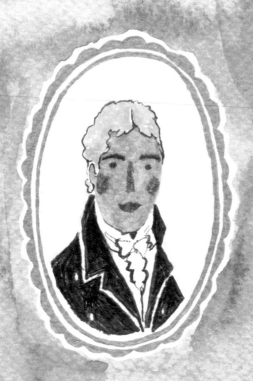

Tom

THEIR ATTRACTION TO EACH OTHER WAS OBVIOUS TO THE NEIGHBORS, AND DESPITE KNOWING HIM ONLY A SHORT TIME, JANE WAS NOT SHY IN PROCLAIMING HER INTEREST IN TOM.

"I am almost afraid to tell you how my Irish friend and I behaved. Imagine to yourself everything most profligate and shocking in the way of dancing and sitting down together."

Letter, January 1796

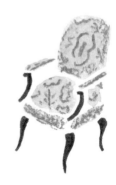

TOM WAS UNDER PRESSURE TO DO
WELL IN HIS CAREER AND MARRY
ADVANTAGEOUSLY. AND JANE WAS A
GIRL WITH NO FORTUNE. AS QUICKLY
AS SHE HAD FALLEN FOR HIM,
HE DISAPPEARED FROM HER LIFE.

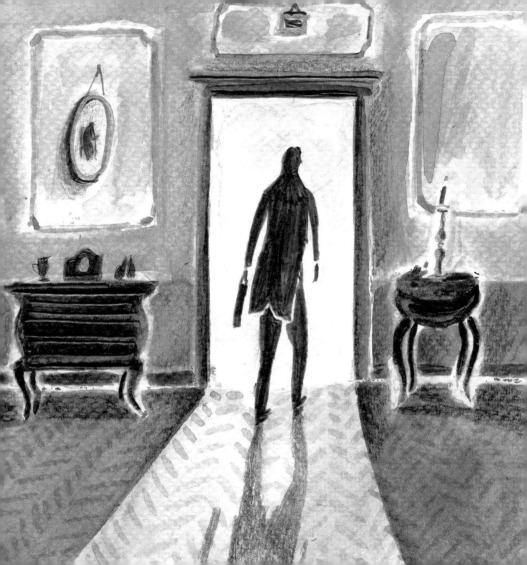

JANE CONTINUED TO WORK STEADILY. BY OCTOBER 1796 SHE HAD BEGUN WRITING "FIRST IMPRESSIONS". WHICH WOULD GO ON TO BECOME "PRIDE AND PREJUDICE". SHE FINISHED THE MANUSCRIPT IN LESS THAN A YEAR AND RETURNED TO "SENSE AND SENSIBILITY" TO RESTRUCTURE AND REVISE IT.

SHE WOULD READ HER WORK
ALOUD TO HER FAMILY.

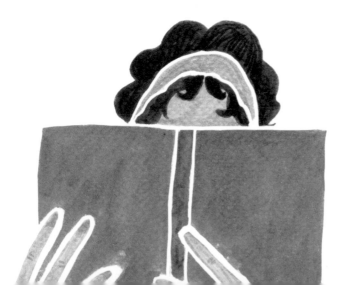

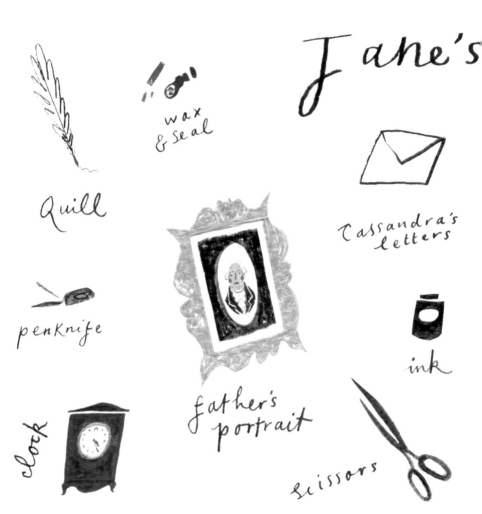

Jane's

Quill

wax & seal

Cassandra's letters

penknife

father's portrait

ink

clock

scissors

Desk

small mirror

lavender

string

spectacles

candlestick

manuscripts

first editions

"SENSE AND SENSIBILITY" WAS ABOUT SISTERS ELINOR AND MARIANNE (ONE DISCREET AND WELL BEHAVED, THE OTHER OPEN AND RECKLESS IN LOVE), AS WELL AS MERCENARY MARRIAGES, CLASS, MONEY, MANIPULATION, AND MANNERS.

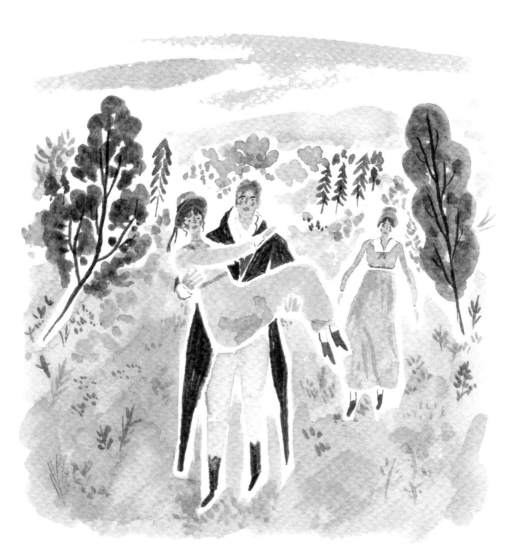

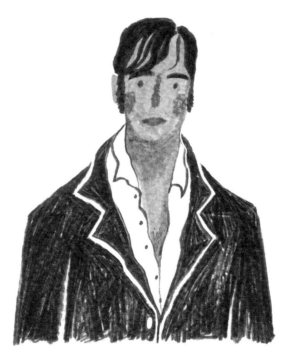

Darcy

"PRIDE AND PREJUDICE" FOLLOWS THE HIGHS AND LOWS OF FIVE BENNET SISTERS, INCLUDING ELIZABETH BENNET, WHO HAS A TURBULENT RELATIONSHIP WITH THE HAUGHTY AND HANDSOME MR. DARCY.

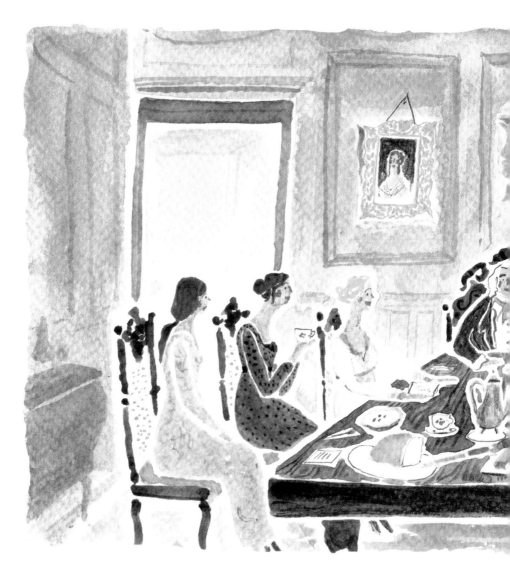

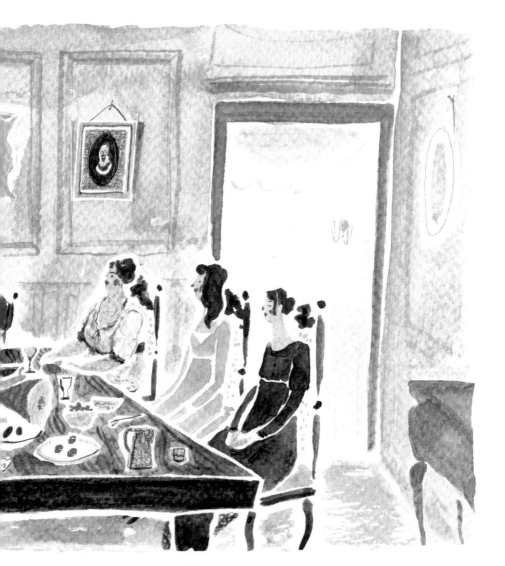

MR. AUSTEN WAS SO PLEASED
WITH HIS DAUGHTER'S MANUSCRIPTS
THAT HE SENT "PRIDE AND
PREJUDICE" TO LONDON PUBLISHER
THOMAS CADELL IN 1797. HE VERY
SWIFTLY RECEIVED AN ANSWER.

Declined
by return of
post

MORE BAD NEWS WAS TO FOLLOW. TO MAKE MONEY FOR HIS FUTURE, CASSANDRA'S BETROTHED HAD BECOME A CHAPLAIN TO AN ENGLISH REGIMENT IN THE WEST INDIES. BUT HE DIED OF YELLOW FEVER BEFORE HE COULD MAKE HIS FORTUNE.

CASSANDRA RECEIVED £1,000
IN HIS WILL.

DEVASTATED BY HER LOST LOVE,
SHE NEVER MARRIED.

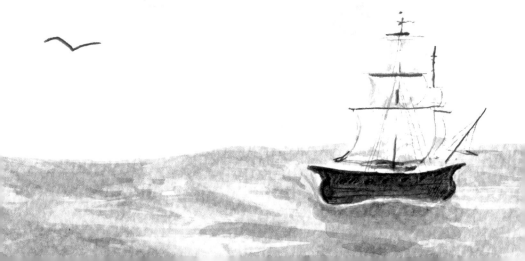

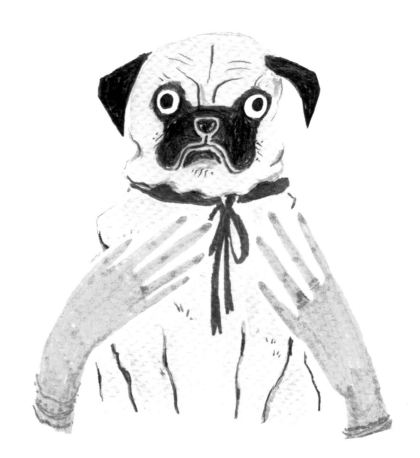

JANE'S BROTHER HENRY, HOWEVER, WAS BUSY COURTING THE STILL EXOTIC, NOW WIDOWED COUSIN ELIZA, AND SUCCEEDED IN WINNING HER HAND.

ELIZA—TEN YEARS HIS SENIOR—ENJOYED THE SOCIAL SCENE AND COULD BE SPOTTED CARRYING HER PUG AROUND LONDON.

ALL AROUND JANE, SMALL FISSURES WERE APPEARING IN THE ESTABLISHED SOCIAL STRUCTURE. MARY WOLLSTONECRAFT'S "VINDICATION OF THE RIGHTS OF WOMAN" (PUBLISHED IN 1792) WAS A CONTROVERSIAL INDICTMENT OF SEXUAL INEQUALITY.

AND JANE WAS A KEEN FAN
OF MORALIST SAMUEL JOHNSON,
WHOSE ESSAYS SUPPORTED SERVICE
TO ONE'S FELLOW MAN AND
DILIGENCE (NOT INHERITANCE) AS
A PATH TO PROSPERITY.

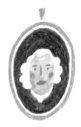

AS HER BROTHERS MARRIED AND HAD
CHILDREN, JANE FELT THE PRESSURE
OF AWKWARD MATCHMAKING. SHE
ALSO HAD THE CHANCE TO OBSERVE
FAMILY LIFE WHILE VISITING HER
BROTHERS AND HELPING WITH HER
MANY NIECES AND NEPHEWS.

JANE BEGAN WORK ON "SUSAN" (LATER KNOWN AS "NORTHANGER ABBEY"). THE ACTION WAS SET IN THE FASHIONABLE RESORT TOWN OF BATH, AND IN 1799 JANE HAD THE CHANCE TO TAKE A TRIP THERE WITH HER MOTHER.

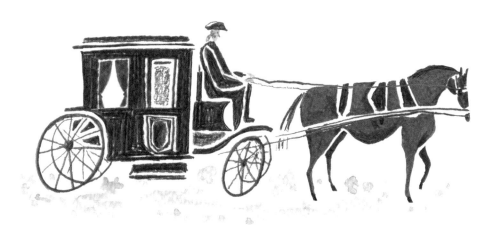

WHENEVER SHE AND CASSANDRA
WERE APART, JANE WROTE REAMS
AND REAMS, FILLING HER SISTER IN
ON DAILY EVENTS.

BUT CASSANDRA DESTROYED
MANY OF JANE'S LETTERS,
ENSURING HER SISTER'S CAUSTIC
JOKES AND CONFIDENTIAL
THOUGHTS REMAINED PRIVATE.

AT THE TURN OF THE CENTURY,
JANE'S PARENTS (NOW IN THEIR
OLD AGE) DECIDED QUITE SUDDENLY
TO LEAVE BEHIND THE RECTORY'S
FARM LIFE IN FAVOR OF THE
PLEASURES OF BATH.

HUNDREDS OF BOOKS WERE SOLD
AND THE HOUSE WAS PACKED UP.

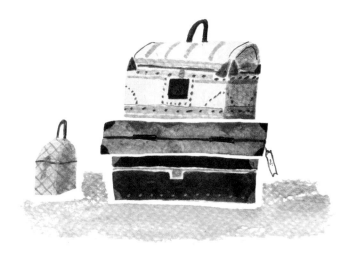

BATH WAS DESIGNED FOR
SOCIALIZING. THERE WERE
THEATER SHOWS AND DANCES,
REJUVENATING WATERS TO
SOAK IN, SHOPS TO VISIT, AND
PARADING GENTRY TO ADMIRE.

PEOPLE-WATCHING WAS ONE OF
BATH'S CHIEF ATTRACTIONS.

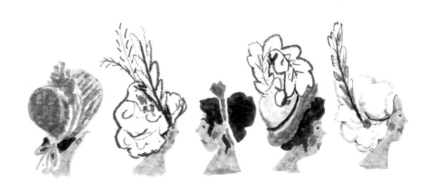

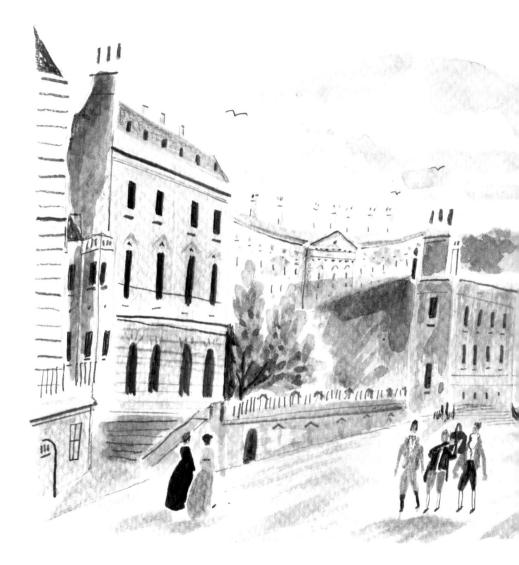

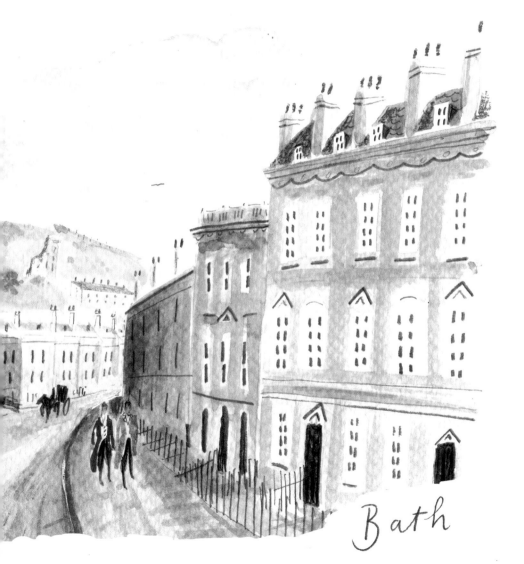

Bath

THE AUSTENS MOVED INTO
4 SYDNEY PLACE, A TERRACED
HOUSE OVERLOOKING PRETTY
GARDENS. DESPITE ITS APPEAL, JANE
WASN'T CONTENT WITH HER NEW
LIFE. IT TOOK HER SEVERAL YEARS
TO RETURN TO HER MANUSCRIPTS.

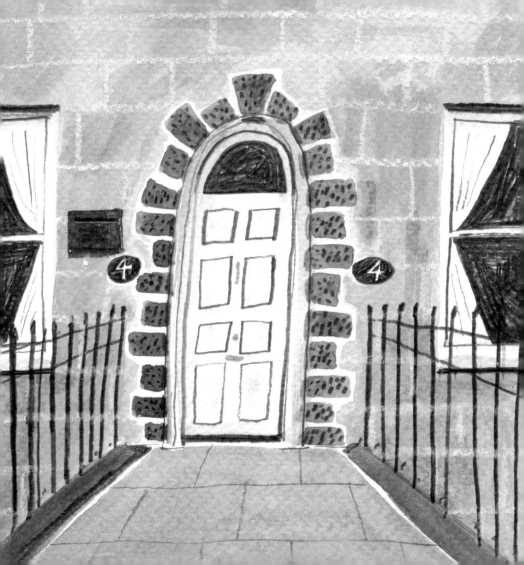

JANE TRIED TO MAKE THE BEST
OF HER NEW SURROUNDINGS.
SHE EXPLORED THE SOUTHWEST
COAST, TRAVELING TO DAWLISH,
TEIGNMOUTH, AND LYME REGIS. SHE
RAMBLED ALONG THE CLIFFS AND
TOOK DIPS IN THE SEA WITH
A BATHING MACHINE.

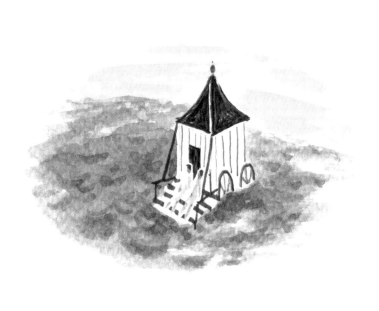

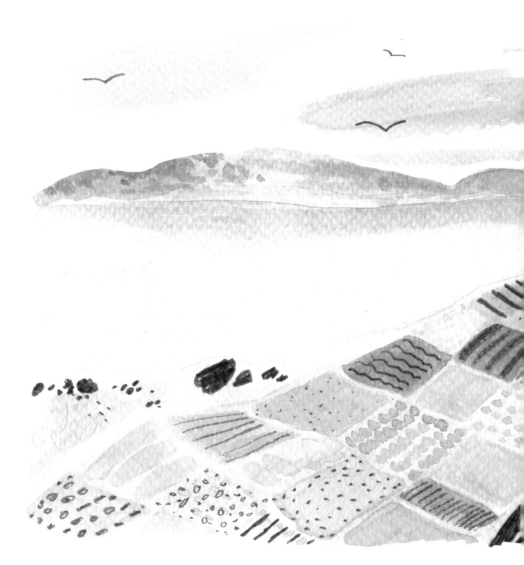

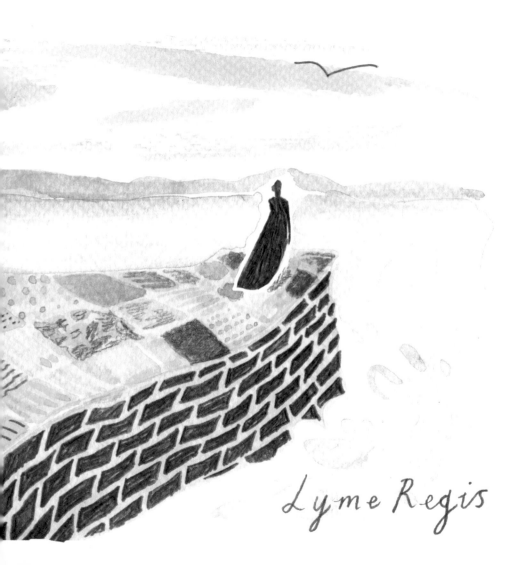

Lyme Regis

ON ONE TRIP, JANE VISITED HER FRIENDS ALETHEA AND CATHERINE BIGG IN HAMPSHIRE, AND SPENT TIME WITH THEIR BROTHER HARRIS.

HARRIS WAS AN AWKWARD YOUNG MAN WITH A STAMMER. HE WAS ALSO HEIR TO A SMALL FORTUNE.

ON DECEMBER 2, 1802,
HARRIS PROPOSED TO JANE.
AND SHE ACCEPTED.

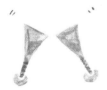

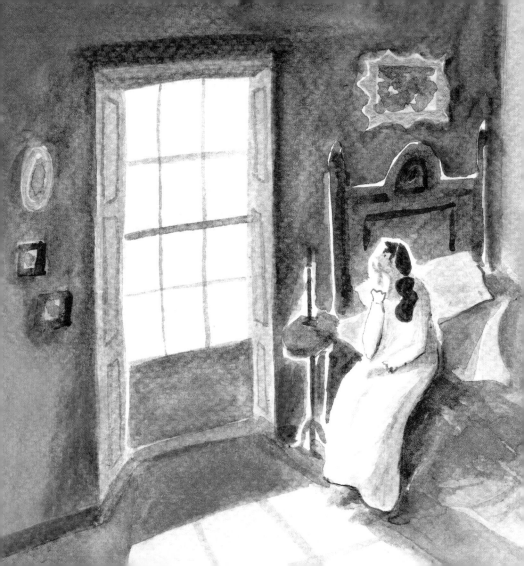

WHEN SHE WOKE THE NEXT DAY,
SHE SOUGHT OUT HARRIS AND
POLITELY EXPLAINED SHE WASN'T
WILLING TO MARRY HIM.

HE FOUND A WIFE TWO YEARS LATER.
SHE BORE HIM TEN CHILDREN.

IN 1803, JANE'S BROTHER HENRY
SENT "NORTHANGER ABBEY" TO
LONDON PUBLISHER RICHARD CROSBY,
WHO AGREED TO A FEE OF £10 FOR
THE BOOK—BUT THEN FAILED
TO PUBLISH IT.

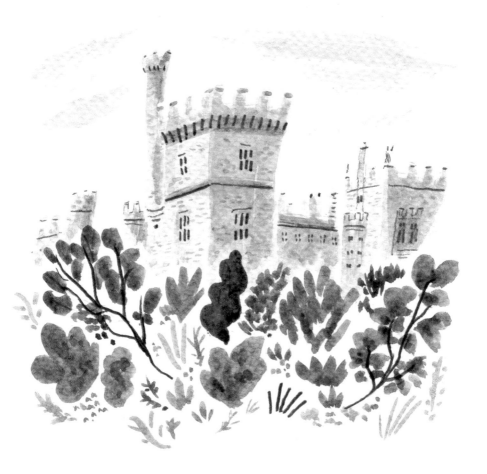

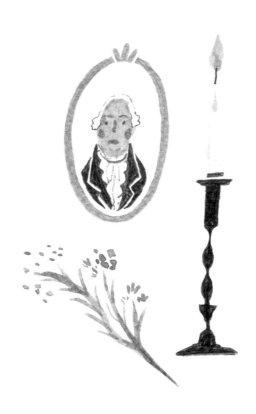

JANE'S SLOWLY RETURNING
ENTHUSIASM FOR WRITING
STALLED AGAIN WHEN HER FATHER
WAS TAKEN ILL AND DIED IN 1805.
HIS DEATH HAD A HUGE IMPACT ON
HIS DEPENDENTS JANE, CASSANDRA,
AND THEIR MOTHER.

THEY WERE COMPELLED TO TAKE
A HOUSE IN SOUTHAMPTON WITH
JANE'S BROTHER FRANK.

LIFE SOON SETTLED DOWN.
JANE'S BROTHER EDWARD OFFERED
HIS MOTHER AND SISTERS A COTTAGE
IN CHAWTON, HAMPSHIRE.

IT HAD SIX BEDROOMS AND A KITCHEN GARDEN. THE AUSTEN WOMEN MOVED THERE IN THE SUMMER OF 1809.

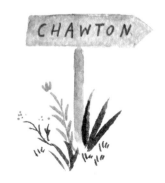

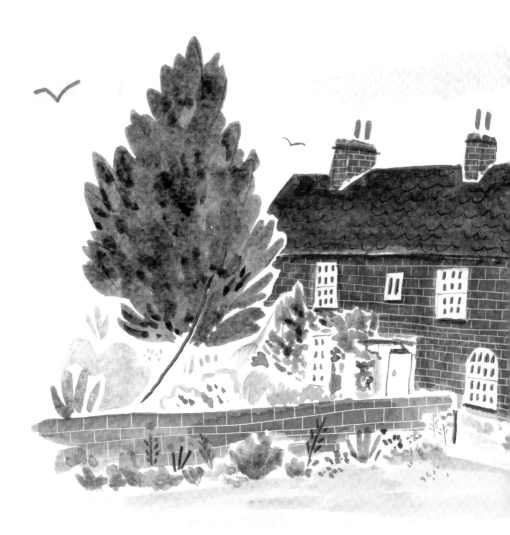

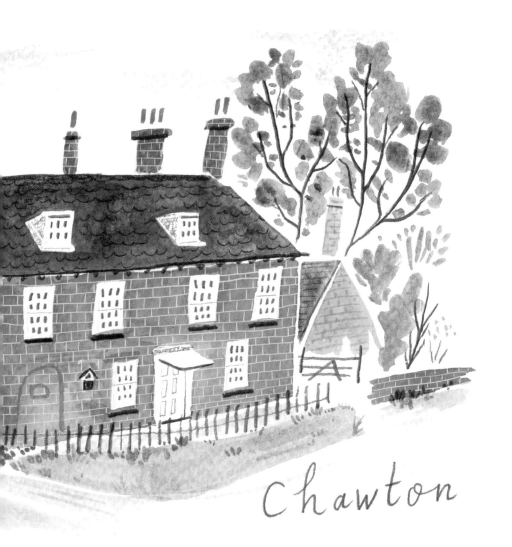

Chawton

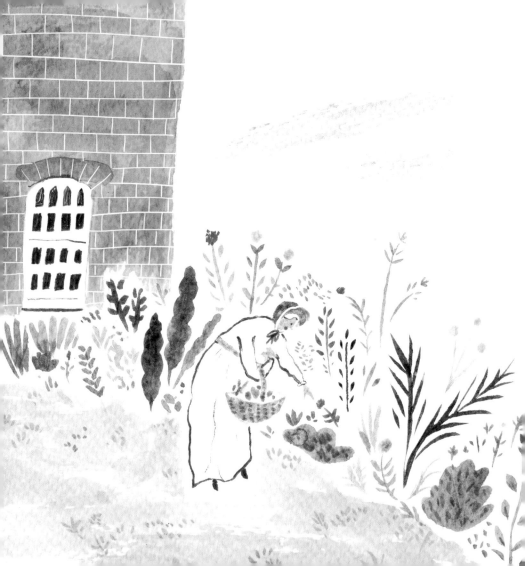

LIFE AT CHAWTON WAS PEACEFUL.
JANE'S MOTHER (NOW IN HER
SEVENTIES) WOULD SPEND HER DAYS
PLANTING POTATOES AND TENDING
TO THE FLOWER BEDS.

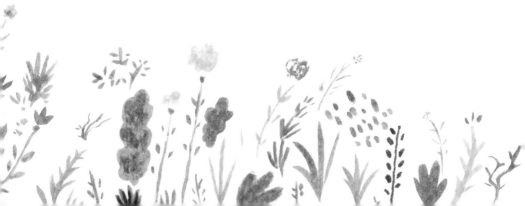

AND JANE WOULD TAKE WALKS
TO NEARBY ALTON, WHERE SHE
WOULD GO SHOPPING WITH HER
SISTER AND POST HER LETTERS.

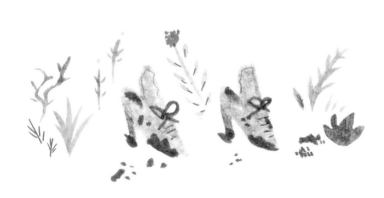

AT CHAWTON JANE FOUND THE CHANCE TO WORK AGAIN. SHE TIDIED UP "SENSE AND SENSIBILITY", AND HENRY FOUND A PUBLISHER WILLING TO PRINT THE BOOK AT THE AUTHOR'S EXPENSE. HENRY AND ELIZA PAID THE COSTS.

THE BOOK, PRICED AT 15
SHILLINGS, SOLD OUT OF ITS FIRST
PRINT RUN. JANE EARNED £140
IN ROYALTIES IN TWO YEARS.

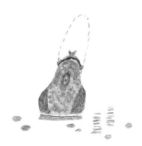

OVER THE NEXT FEW YEARS,
JANE MADE SEVERAL VISITS
TO HENRY AND ELIZA'S HOUSE
ON SLOANE STREET IN LONDON.
SHE TOOK WALKS TO THE CENTER
OF TOWN AND CARRIAGE RIDES
TO THE THEATER.

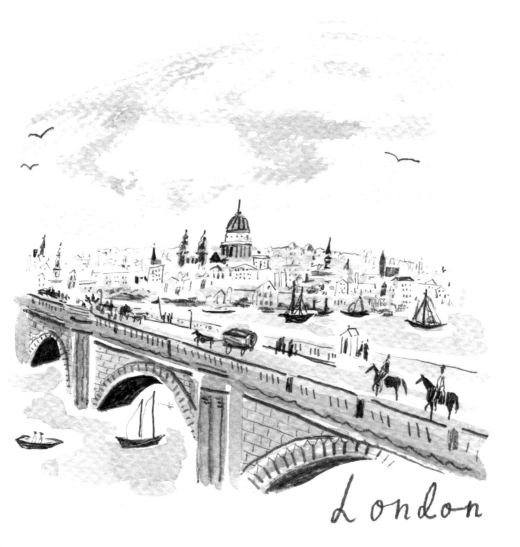

London

JANE PUBLISHED ANONYMOUSLY, AND HER LIFE AT CHAWTON CONTINUED UNDISTURBED. HER DAILY DUTY WAS TO MAKE A BREAKFAST OF TEA AND TOAST ON THE FIRE. SHE WOULD WAKE UP EARLY AND PRACTICE AT THE PIANO BEFORE THE REST OF THE HOUSEHOLD STIRRED.

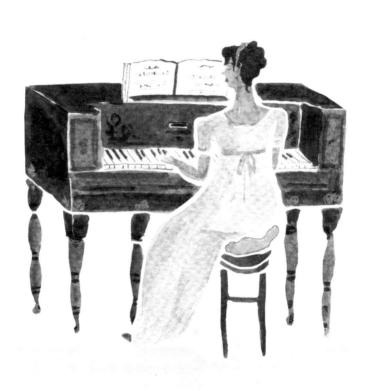

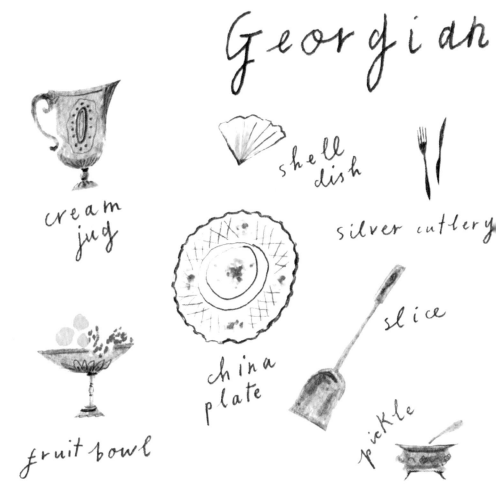

Georgian

cream
jug

shell
dish

silver cutlery

china
plate

slice

pickle

fruit bowl

Dining

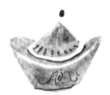

mustard
pot

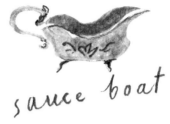

sauce boat

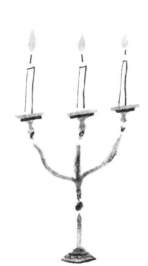

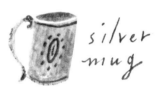

silver
mug

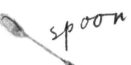
spoon

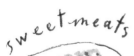

sweetmeats

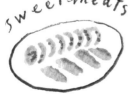

candelabra

teacup

teapot

IN 1811, SHE BEGAN WORK ON
"MANSFIELD PARK". THE NOVEL
CENTERED AROUND FANNY PRICE,
A YOUNG LADY WITH HIGH MORALS
AND NO INCOME. THRUST INTO THE
UPPER ECHELONS OF SOCIETY, FANNY
REMAINS STOIC IN THE FACE OF
FRIVOLITY AND TEMPTATION.

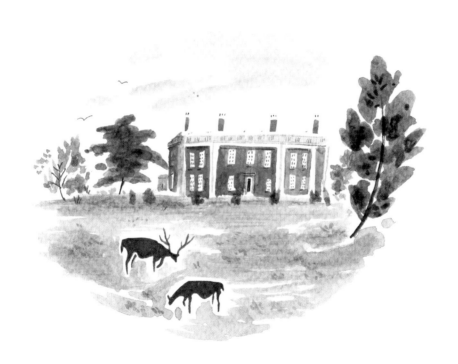

BUOYED BY THE CRITICAL SUCCESS OF "SENSE AND SENSIBILITY" AND ITS POPULARITY AMONG THE RICH AND FASHIONABLE, JANE OFFERED THE SAME PUBLISHER (THOMAS EGERTON OF THE MILITARY LIBRARY) THE COPYRIGHT TO "PRIDE AND PREJUDICE" IN 1812.

THE BOOK SOLD TO THE PUBLIC FOR
18 SHILLINGS. SHE RECEIVED £110.

READERS FELL IN LOVE WITH
ELIZABETH BENNET. AND JANE WAS
PARTIAL TO THE CHARACTER, TOO.

"i must confess that i think her
as delightful a creature as ever
appeared in print, how i shall be able to
tolerate those who do not like her
at least, i do not know."

Letter, january 1813

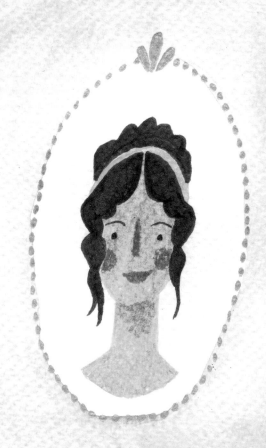

ELIZABETH

JANE MOVED SWIFTLY ON TO HER
NEXT HEROINE, STARTING "EMMA"
IN EARLY 1814 AND FINISHING THE
NOVEL IN SPRING 1815, JUST AS
"MANSFIELD PARK" WAS PUBLISHED.

"EMMA" WAS A COMEDY OF
ERRORS REVOLVING AROUND
ILL-ADVISED MATCHMAKING AND
MISGUIDED MANIPULATION.

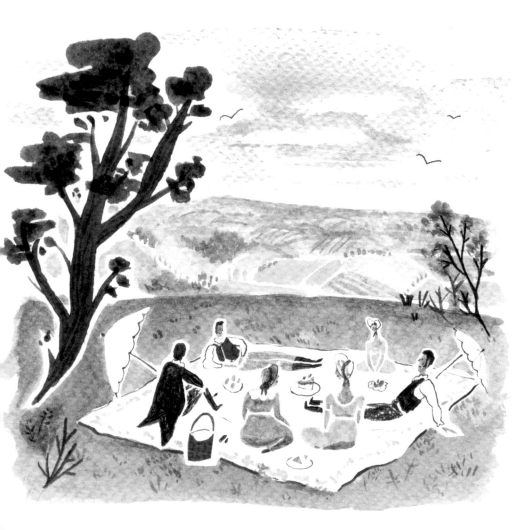

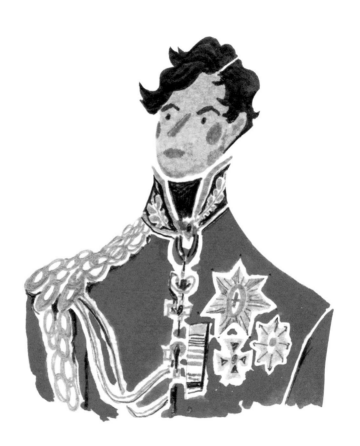

JANE'S IDENTITY AS AN AUTHOR
WAS GRADUALLY REVEALED, AND THE
PRINCE REGENT DECLARED HIMSELF
A FAN. HE MADE IT KNOWN THAT
HE WANTED JANE TO DEDICATE
"EMMA" TO HIM.

AS JANE TURNED FORTY IN
DECEMBER 1815, TWO THOUSAND
COPIES OF "EMMA" WERE PRINTED
(COMPLETE WITH A DEDICATION
TO THE ROYAL ADMIRER). THE BOOK
SOLD FOR 21 SHILLINGS.

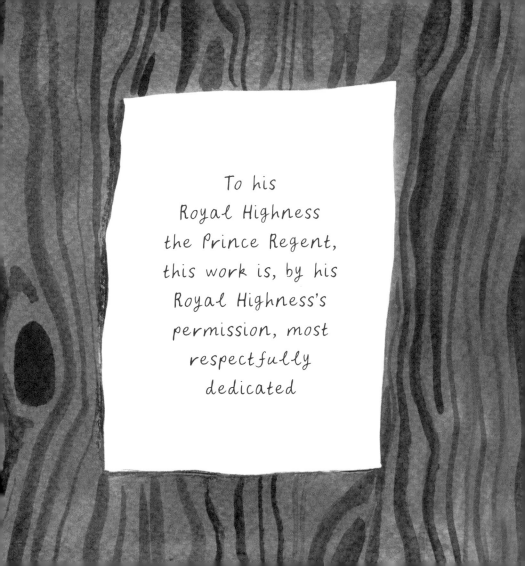

To his
Royal Highness
the Prince Regent,
this work is, by his
Royal Highness's
permission, most
respectfully
dedicated

AFTER THIS FLURRY OF PUBLISHING
TRIUMPHS, CRITICAL SUCCESS,
AND MODEST FAME, JANE BEGAN
TO FEEL UNWELL. SHE KEPT BUSY
WRITING "THE ELLIOTS", WHICH
WENT ON TO BECOME "PERSUASION".
BUT IT WOULD BE PUBLISHED
POSTHUMOUSLY.

"PERSUASION" WAS AS CLOSELY OBSERVED AS JANE'S PREVIOUS NOVELS. HEROINE ANNE ELLIOT WAS A YOUNG WOMAN TALKED OUT OF MARRYING A MAN DEEMED TOO LOWLY FOR HER, ONLY TO MEET HIM SOME TEN YEARS LATER AS A RICH, SUCCESSFUL, AND ADMIRED NAVY CAPTAIN.

DESPITE HER REFUSAL TO
ADMIT SERIOUS ILLNESS, JANE WAS
SOON CONFINED TO HER BED. IN
APRIL 1817 SHE PRIVATELY WROTE
HER WILL AND SOON AFTER WAS
TAKEN TO LODGINGS AT 8 COLLEGE
STREET IN WINCHESTER TO BE NEAR
HER SURGEON.

"if i live to be an old woman i must expect to wish i had died now, blessed in the tenderness of such a family, before i survived either them or their affection."

Letter, May 1817

ON JULY 18, 1817, JANE
DIED PEACEFULLY WITH HER HEAD
RESTING ON HER SISTER'S LAP.
SHE WAS FORTY-ONE.

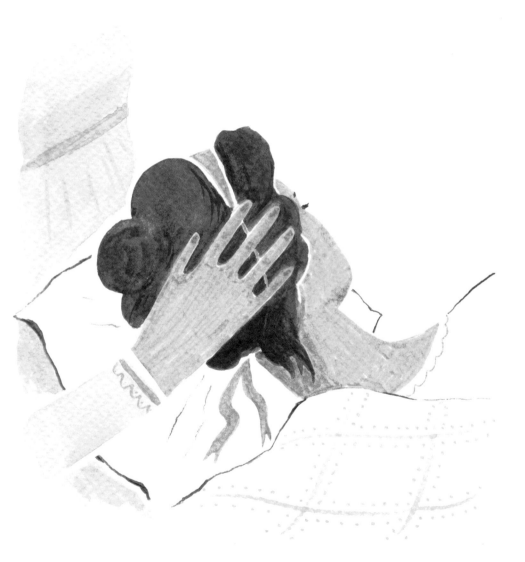

"She was the sun of my life,
the gilder of every pleasure,
the soother of every sorrow."

Cassandra Austen, July 1817

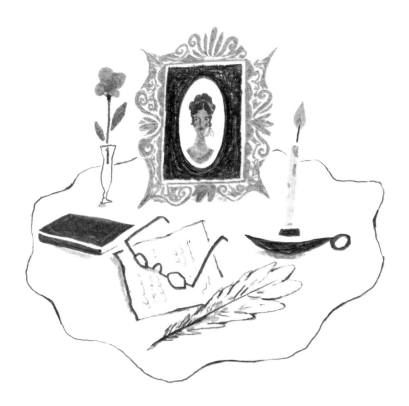

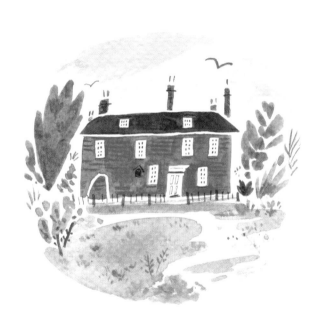

Acknowledgments

The author gratefully acknowledges the
information and inspiration provided
by Claire Tomalin's wonderful biography
Jane Austen: A Life. Further thanks
go to Joan Strasbaugh, author of *The List
Lover's Guide to Jane Austen*, for her
consultation on the book. Her expertise
was invaluable.

The illustrator would like to extend her
love and thanks to Ali, Ma, Pops, Jojo,
and Chester.

The quotations used in this publication
have been sourced from the following:

Jane Austen's Letters, ed. Deirdre Le Faye
(Oxford University Press).

Selected Letters, ed. Vivien Jones
(Oxford University Press).

Pride and Prejudice, Jane Austen
(Penguin).

About the authors

Zena Alkayat is a bestselling author, book editor, and journalist from London. With many years of experience in media and publishing, she has covered subjects from tea and cake to concrete, cocktails, and Coco Chanel.

Nina Cosford is a freelance illustrator based in the southeast of England. She works across editorial, advertising, education, typography, and book illustration and has created work for clients from Nokia to *Marie Claire*.

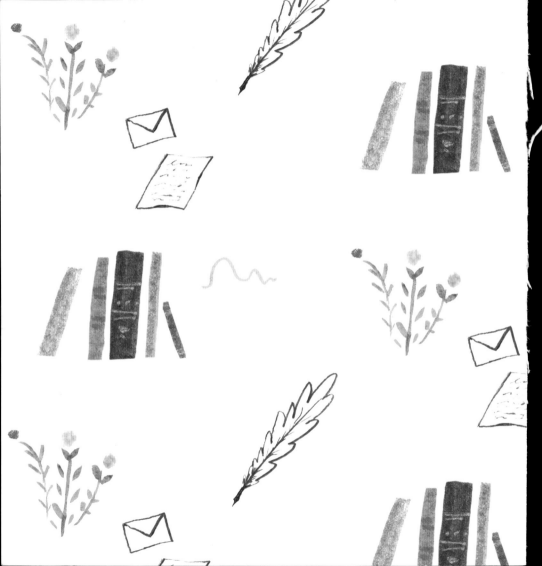